Phoenix Rising

Phoenix Rising

Lee Gray

Published by Lee Gray, 2023.

PHOENIX RISING

First edition. December 20, 2023.

ISBN: 979-8230455585

Written by Lee Gray.

For Maly.

Like Poem

This isn't a love poem.
This is a like poem.
I
really like you.
Your energy is like water,
cool blue water,
standing still,
or lapping gently at my feet
whenever you want me.
And I am here when you want me,
because you like me too.
It would be an honor to be needed.
Sweet and distant goddess,
it would be an honor to be loved by you.

Helpless

I imagine if you touched me,
my insides would collapse like dominoes,
and you,
sweet and merciful thing,
would pour me into a cup,
until I had collected myself.
I imagine if you kissed me,
I would tumble apart
like a shower of candies
when a glass jar has broken—
I would shatter into a thousand colored pebbles,
I would burst on your tongue,
and you would taste me and know delight.
In your arms, in your arms
you would gather me to your breasts.
And doesn't it feel right?
Oh.
How helpless am I rendered.
Gentle goddess,
I surrender.

I'm Worthy

I'm ready for love.
I'm ready.
I'm worthy. I'm worthy now.
And it's ironic,
so painfully ironic.
When I had a home,
when I had a job,
when I was in shape,
when I had direction—
I was not ready.
I was miserable.
I was a prisoner of my own mind,
breathing in thorns
and exhaling needles,
tortured by my past,
dark and angry. . . . and made of glass.
Then I lost my job and I became
Homeless.
Homeless. The word like a bad taste in my mouth—
And now there's so much clarity.
The thorns and needles are gone, carried off on the wind,
and though I'm still alone,
There is only . . . peace. I don't need a friend.
I don't cry myself to sleep.
I don't rage against the injustice of my childhood abuse.
I . . . listen to music. I meditate. I pray. I draw. I smile. I sleep well.
What the . . . utter hell?
It took losing everything—
everything!—
to gain everything.
And the irony,
the painful IRONY

is now that I'm mentally, emotionally well,
I'm also homeless,
and women's eyes, when they look at me,
show only pity.
Sometimes smugness. THEY could never be homeless.
Sometimes disgust.
Sometimes lust.
But all their eyes, their stares, their glances,
say I am unworthy of love—
when I have never been so worthy of love—
And I wonder if anyone will ever really look at me,
ever really SEE me
again.

Dear Hypothetical Girlfriend

Dear girlfriend I haven't dated yet,
dear woman I never loved,
who has not yet loved me,
you exist in half-dreams,
sending chemicals of lust
and delight to my brain.
You walk with hips I never
shaped in my hands,
breasts I have never caressed,
a sex I have never enjoyed the heat and moisture of against my eager lips –
I awoke thinking of you,
of the rose petals on our bed
at every anniversary,
of inside jokes whispered in public
as you laugh and pat my arm,
of your pride that you have a sweet, sensitive, girlfriend
who writes romance novels for a living,
who doesn't take shit from anyone,
who leaves you paper cranes with hidden love notes in your shoes,
who couldn't conceive of making love to another woman,
who thinks the world of you.
The gold wedding band already exists that I will wear the rest of life,
future wife,
I dream of you.
I haven't even met you,
and already, I'm on Cloud Nine,
thinking of all the love I could give,
of all the love that would be mine.
Of course, when we met it will be something . . . mundane.
You will ask me for directions,
or we'll we be standing in the same elevator,
or you'll drop a book and I'll hand it back to you—and *boop*. Attraction.

All those Love At First Sight chemicals going off in our brains,
dates leading to laughter to kisses to love—
But again, the first meeting would have to be mundane.
Life isn't a romance novel.

Dis.con.nect

I've
lost the ability
to connect with people.
I'm slipping away.
I'm alone.
Alone. In a sea of faces.
I
have to carve out spaces
so I can breathe.
There's no room for me
In this shithole they call the world—
"Ma',am, you can't just be sitting at the bus stop—"
And I move.
So these
rich assholes eating cantaloupe and sour cream at the sandwich shop don't have to look at me.
He wouldn't have known I was homeless
if I weren't forced to overdress for the winter.
But they all know.
Alone.
So alone. Because no one can be trusted.
But I'm not sad.
I
have become an impartial bystander observing my own life.
I'm addicted
to fantasies—
Too busy dreaming of my house on the beach to be lonely,
To be sad,
To be mad—
"Do you need help, sweetheart?" she asks, because it's Christmas, because I seem not to be crazy or high.
But I barely hear her.

I’m listening to music,
I’m sunning on the beach,
I’m not even fucking here.

Anniversary

Today
is my one-year anniversary
of homelessness.
Today
a man walked by me
and said what sounded like my name,
and I thought,
"Holy shit, how does he know my name?"
And I realized,
"Holy shit, that's my name."
It's been so long since someone called me
by name.
It's been a year.
You see,
I don't talk to people anymore.
I don't tell people my name.
No one knows me and no one wants to know—
Except predatory men
who demand that I divulge this secret,
as if they were princes and kings
and I a lowly peasant girl ripe for raping.
I tell them my name is not their fucking business.
But they want my name.
Names have power.
So I remain
the stranger who you cross the street to avoid,
carrying her entire life in a bags—
The nothing.
The nobody.
And it only took one year
to fall off the edge of society and forget myself—
Erasing myself

like one of my bad paintings—
Roll the gesso over my name, smooth like the rain falling over my tent.
Forget me. Gone. Forgotten. Rotten.
And it only took one year.
My name,
a distant memory.
Now how long before the rest of me?

Goodnight

I always feel better,
after the nightly ritual,
after holding child's pose—
It sends me back
to the dark of Mother's womb
before I knew
Mother as Monster—
I lie in my tent,
knowing I never had a mother,
who cared about my nightmares,
who sang me to sleep—
The sound of the city
has become my lullaby,
my tent has become the womb.
Happy chatter,
people swearing and screaming,
so much angry Spanish,
cars roaring by,
music booming,
and somehow, I sleep,
curled inside my sleeping bag,
in my tent,
I have grown accustomed to the music of the night,
so desperate for rest, I.
Sing to me, junky.
Tell me a bedtime story, crazy man,
who nightly rounds the block screaming—
Could anyone love me
if they knew
what my soul has been through?
My wife,
she exists in dreams.

This fictional lover can see
the fire blazing in my homeless heart.
Goodnight.
Goodnight.
I'll keep a light on.

And There She Was

It's a trite saying, but it's true:
love always comes when you stop caring.
I said, "There's no such thing as love."
I said, "I'll never give my heart to a woman again."
I said, "I'm too dead inside to want anyone."
And I deleted my poetry from Instagram.
And I closed my eyes.
And I closed my heart.
I decided
alone was how I'd always been
and alone was how I'd always be—
And there she was,
the most beautiful thing I'd ever seen,
out of nowhere,
she stood before me,
and my brain lost all its functioning,
all its reason,
as happy chemicals collided inside it—
She greets me with a smile.
I, dullard, can't form a sentence, she must think I'm challenged—
But there she was,
a beautiful butch woman,
but so soft and pretty,
a gentle lavender flame obscuring the rest of the world—
the rest of my world—
With the gentlest whisper,
with the gentlest touch,
she has brought me to my knees.
How is she there?
How was she real?
And how did she steal
my beating heart from my chest

without my even noticing?
There she goes, walking off with it,
and I follow like a puppy dog.
I look at her, and I know,
this woman will destroy me, ruin me, undo me
like all the others.
But I have no choice—
no choice, for I am required by law—
to see her again and again,
to melt again and again.
God above, what cruel, cruel jest,
that I should cross paths with her
and know no rest?
Another woman I can't have, can't love, can't kiss,
dangled in my face,
while I dangle from the noose of homelessness.
Oh, what BLISS
is sweetest life.

Stray

You know those shirts that say,
"My Dog Thinks I'm Cool"?
That's kinda how it feels to be homeless, I think.
Always hated,
always on the brink
of losing your sanity—
And then a dog "smiles" at you.
At least dogs still love you.
I have had people's dogs
jump randomly in my lap,
rise on hind legs and stand against my legs
while waiting happily to be patted,
drag their owners to me on the end of their leash to say hello,
burst upon me randomly and kiss me—
And it's so funny
to see the owners of these dogs panicking,
so terrified that the scary homeless person will harm their "fur baby."
But the dogs aren't afraid.
The dogs know.
The dogs know I will pet them, smile at them, be kind to them,
that I don't mind if they sit on my lap.
I don't know what it is about dogs,
but they always peg harmless people.
The smart ones, anyway.
This morning I was sitting outside,
I was drawing and enjoying the sunlight.
A man's dog insisted on coming over to look at me,
and curiously enough, the man allowed this.
I was startled to look up and find them both standing there.
The dog had a sort of pitying expression like, "Where is your owner?"
"Why are you out here alone, human?"
"Are you a stray? Have they abandoned you?"

Yes, my furry friend.
I am a stray. They abandoned me.
California will never let a dog live in desperation on the streets, you see.
But a human living in the gutter? Well, that's just fine and dandy.
The human deserves it. The human is evil. The homeless are evil by default.
We deserve to live like beasts.
Right? Isn't that the natural order?
The rich are virtuous, and the poor are wicked? Or something.
And imagine explaining this to a dog,
a dog that looks at you
and doesn't understand why you have been abandoned by your pack.
There is no explaining.
Just know, little doggy, that lone wolves, we exist.
Now run along. Live your happy days with your master in the sun.
Leave me to shuffle through the ruins of my life.

Civility

I bend over the fountain for a drink,
but I stop and stare.
A slug,
a garden slug
is already there.
It winds itself over the faucet,
extends its feelers inquisitively.
I oblige, pressing the button so it may drink.
Water sparkles in the early light of day.
First come, first served.
It had the right of way.

Not This Time

You're just like all the others—
Another
woman who I could love,
who can't love me.
I knew it when I saw you.
The very MOMENT I saw you.
My brain screeched.
It knew. It knew better.
But my heart proceeded.
And without caution.
We can't help who we love.
We can't stop the chemicals that burst in the brain,
the shortness of breath,
the stirring of the loins,
the rain
of sudden emotion.
But not this time.
Not this time.
NOT THIS TIME.
I will NOT
pour my cup
and stand with it empty,
stand there and die of thirst,
while you bask in my drooling.
I will NOT
chase you like a fool.
You will NOT
be my undoing.
I will NOT
wait for you to suddenly feel the same.
I will NOT
fantasize.

I will NOT
weep and wane.
You cannot love me beyond your lust and attraction,
so I will lift my head and move on,
dignity intact.

Lonely No More

I have found the cure to loneliness.
Are you ready?
It's no longer needing outside validation.
It's no longer caring if people accept you,
love you, like you,
want you around.
It's the elation
of realizing you are all you need,
that you are enough,
that other people's opinions are just . . . extra stuff.
Like toppings on ice cream.
Being lonely is like only wanting the toppings on ice cream
but having no ice cream to put them on.
I mean, who doesn't love gummy bears in their ice cream?
But you need to have ice cream first,
and you can live without the gummy bears.
The ice cream won't taste as good, sure,
but it's fucking ice cream. It will always taste good.
You are fucking ice cream. You don't NEED toppings to be delectable.
I am delectable. I don't need people to know that.
Years and years of trying to get to this place of
self-acceptance
and one day it just hit me like a bolt out of the blue—
FUCK ALL OF YOU. I am enough.
I don't need external validation.
I am enough. I am enough. I am enough!
Something I only ever heard from Mr. Rodgers growing up
finally registers in my brain.
I am enough,
and all my pain,
all the agony I put myself through,
because I believed I was unlovable,

was pointless, pointless—
a prison my mother placed me in,
a prison the bullies placed me in,
a prison emotionally abusive lovers placed me in,
and I chose to stay.
But now I'm okay.
I don't need other people to love me. I love me.
Yes. It finally happened – I love me!
And
there's no feeling like it in the world.

Nothing I Can Do

Why can't I stop thinking of you?
I am half annoyed and half helpless.
You're a stranger,
yet you intrude upon my thoughts,
enclosing me in your arms from behind,
as if you had done so a thousand times before,
under a thousand different suns,
in a thousand different skins,
gazing at me across time from behind a thousand different eyes—
And in each incarnation, I was your wife—
Your eyes
are so familiar.
I felt safe,
when you touched me that day,
I felt alive.
Then I began to crave you.
You didn't do it on purpose, but you did it,
made me want you, made me miss you, made me light up when I'm with you.
Made me want to kiss you.
Your fingers touching my back
made me think of your fingers touching my lips.
The lips below my hips.
And now out of nowhere,
my mind is a whirl of us kissing—
You turn my face toward you,
and our lips embrace,
and your insistent hands
touch my breasts,
and I'm a mess
wondering how this happened,
wondering how to make it stop,
feeling helpless to make it stop,

(secretly wishing it never stops).
"Don't stop
touching me," I wanted to say that day.
"Don't take
your hands from my body," I wanted to plea.
Only you . . .
can make me plea . . .
It was such an innocent gesture when you touched me.
And I need,
I need to know what it's like
to have those hands touch my bare skin
and bring it to life.
You aren't mine. I have no right . . .
I have no right to you.
I have no right to feel this way.
I have no right to think these thoughts.
But I crave you.
And there is nothing I can do.
Nothing I can do
but dream of you.

Releasing the Fear

What if you're nothing like my former lovers?
What if you're actually single?
What if you actually wanted me,
wanted to commit to me
and only me?
What if we were happy?
What if we fell in love?
What if we stayed together,
happy and content for years,
and what if all my fears
were trauma induced bullshit?
What if you were the best thing that ever happened to me?
What if I gave you my tender heart
and you didn't break it?
What if I was naked
and you loved my body?
Consumed my body?
Adored my body?
What if everything was beautiful and wonderful like a fucking fairytale?
What if I stopped being afraid for six seconds?
Why, I just might experience love.

Grrrrreat

My neck is killing me.
I slept sideways
with my head on my duffel bag,
and I dreamt
of an ordinary day in our life together.
You sipping coffee,
me your housewife.
We are so normal,
it makes the word "queer" ironic,
as if gay people were beasts at the zoo—
Curiosities at the circus for the straights to ponder—
Us living our ordinary lives behind glass.
I hand you a packed lunch.
You kiss my cheek.
"Have a GRRRREAT day, honey!"
You laugh. It's an inside joke. We have those.
"I love you."
I watch you drive away,
and there's a gold wedding band on my finger.
I say a prayer for your safe return,
for your safety throughout the day,
I pray.
God grants your return, and we make love.
All night, we make love.
That is my dream.
In reality, I don't know what real love is.
I only know what love isn't.
Would that be enough?
Me cooking you supper and listening to your day—
because it's the best part of my day—
Would it be love?
Is love an action?

Is love a chemical going off in our brains?
Is it both?
I don't know.
I only know that I dream of what could be
when I am sleeping on my duffel bag.
It is nice to dream.
It is nice to imagine
that someone could love me.
And that it would be great.

By Being You

I dream of you
on top of me,
soft hot skin
crushing
soft hot skin,
and you're inside,
inside of me,
and all the world stands still
as we kiss,
as I arch my back beneath you and moan—
Just how deep
can your fingers go?
And will you ever know
how much my body craves you?
Has always craved you,
since the moment I met you?
I can't . . .
forget you.
And it's taking me over.
We kiss as we make love,
smile into each other's eyes,
laugh together,
breasts trembling against breasts,
and I wonder,
is it too good to be true?
Will these dreams
ever come to pass?
Or will they stay forever dreams?
I don't know, and it frightens me.
But I know one thing:
I miss the sound of your voice,
and your touch,

and your eyes smiling into my eyes.
I miss how you made me laugh—
Not when you tried to be funny,
but when you didn't try to be funny—
I miss having you near.
And . . . it's not a terrible feeling.
I am not in deepest despair.
I am not falling to pieces
because you are not there.
I just . . . miss you.
And it feels good
to dream of kissing you.
You have only ever made me feel good.
To desire you,
to long for you,
to miss you—
This is what it is
to be a lesbian,
to be a gay woman in a gay woman's body,
with a woman's soft skin,
and with a woman's warm thighs,
with a woman's breasts,
with a woman's smiling eyes—
With a woman's loving heart—
With a woman's lust.
And I must
never let this feeling go.
It's a natural part of me,
and you stirred it,
woke me from slumber
with a metaphorical kiss.
Just by being you.
That's the part you miss.
You think that I think so little of you.
But I liked you before you ever opened your mouth.

Before you spoke a word,
I looked up,
and the chemicals went off in my brain as I beheld you—
You, this beautiful butch woman.
I felt it,
every part of my body
screaming
for your body.
And you didn't have to do anything,
be anything,
change anything.
Just by being you. Just by being you.
God. If only you knew.

Be Real

And still,
this feeling persists,
this
desire to be kissed
and held by you.
You put me in feminine energy.
I am always longing
to be under you,
held by you,
touched by you,
kissed by you.
And it's not a bad thing.
My ex always wanted me to top her,
to dominate her,
to do things to her,
saw the tomboy in me and decided I should give
and never receive.
No one has ever cared about giving me pleasure,
or love,
or affection,
or even her protection.
I was a toy.
A fantasy.
She . . . didn't care about ME.
But I can feel it in your gaze,
how I know you would love me,
hold me,
protect me,
and let me love you in return.
I can feel it in your gaze,
how you
yearn

for me.
Are you the one I've been waiting for?
I confess, I'm afraid.
I'm afraid to believe it's real.
Heartache springs eternal
from disappointment.
Please, be real.
Be real and not
a fantasy or projection.
Be real and not
lies and rejection.
I'm so tired of disappointment.
Can things just be beautiful and wonderful . . .
just once?

Rubber Ducky

It's been a while.
I keep trying to forget you,
then I think of you and smile.
The other day I saw a rubber ducky,
and I laughed.
Laughed out loud in public.
People must've thought I was mad,
the homeless woman,
giggling to herself,
rocking back and forth with laughter.
But the rubber ducky reminded me of us
and how we both love the damn things.
Of course, our tastes vary.
You like the novelty ones with red lipstick.
I like the classic ones,
like Ernie in the bath.
Rubber Ducky, you're the one—
Are you the one?
Probably not.
You're probably not looking for a commitment,
or you have a busy life,
or you have a wife—
That's how it always goes,
my inner child,
forever drawn to women who can't love her,
because Mother couldn't love her,
refusing to listen no matter how many times I tell her
we are worthy of love,
we are worthy of reciprocity.
She doesn't understand reciprocity.
She was raised to believe love has conditions, you see.
But you and me,

even if we can't be,
I can see us in the bath together.
Foamy bubbles wobble on the surface of the water.
The soap slips through my fingers.
My breasts slip through your fingers.
And as we kiss,
the rubber duckies bob, forgotten, on the water.
Rubber Ducky,
you're the one.
And
I'm awfully fond of you.

I Would Wear Yellow

If I weren't homeless,
if I could choose how to spend my days,
I would wear sundresses,
in vibrant colors of pink and yellow—
I would no longer fear the fade of the sun,
the mark of stains
the rain—
I would wear yellow,
loud, happy, silly, bright yellow—
Announcing to the world that this is who I am,
and if you don't like it,
seethe.
This is me.
In yellow sundresses and wide-brimmed straw hats,
walking happily through my wild garden,
watering my plants,
smiling under wind-chimes
and colorful bottles that hang on strings.
This is me
doing yoga in tight yoga pants,
unafraid to be who I am.
Fruit smoothies and grilled cheese sandwiches.
I fall asleep listening to the rain,
no longer having to fear hypothermia
or arthritic pain—
Me
finally happy and free of all suffering.
Me
no longer having to fend off male lusting.
Herbal tea and long hot baths.
Tree pose.
Surrounded by house plants.

Lock the door and be safe.
Goodbye to the vulnerability of my tent on the street.
I would sing
and smile
and dance with happy feet,
without fear of attracting male violence—
And the silence. I would close the door,
and no more
screaming junkies,
no more
loud swearing and cars roaring by.
Just me
in silence so precious I cry.
Finally alone,
finally alone and at peace,
finally able to let down my hair,
and homelessness a distant nightmare.
No more sadness, anguish, and despair,
for I would wear yellow.
God, I would wear yellow.
And those who wished to hurt me wouldn't dare.

Earrings

Homeless woman,
you are not allowed to be beautiful,
you are not allowed to wear beautiful things,
to wear color,
to shine,
but I sat on the internet,
and I looked a long time
at those earrings.
Glistening gold hoops
with turquoise beads
and cowrie shells.
How long before they broke,
bent,
became filthy?
How long before I break,
bend,
remain filthy—
filthy for the rest of my days?
How long before the endless maze
of despair takes over me?
And can I stop the tidal wave?
Can I be brave
and live another day?
Can I be brave
and wear gold hoops—
sparkling in the sun,
winking,
a mating call,
a siren saying,
"Look at me!"
I dare,
I dare to be vulnerable and beautiful.

Look and see.
How I dare,
I dare to be me.

I Just Want You

I hate myself for this,
for wanting you,
for missing you.
Why?
You're a STRANGER.
We met twice,
two ships passing in the night,
except our sails became tangled—
By fate,
by circumstance,
by chance—
We dance under the moon,
and I can still feel it,
your hand on my back,
touching my back.
I wonder what else those can hands can do?
I try to move on,
I try to fantasize about someone else,
I try to imagine anyone else,
but you're still there.
You.
Ever looming over my shoulder.
I just want you.
And I shouldn't.
And we shouldn't.
And the cost is too high.
But if I don't kiss you
perhaps I'll die.

Fingers

I've wanted your fingers inside me
since the moment I met you.
I know you can feel it,
how I can't forget you.
I'm wet for you,
yet blazing inside.
I'm an inferno,
yet moist in your fingers—
Your hungry gaze lingers.
Your kiss shall be my doom.
Your fingers coax me to life.
My flower is in bloom.

Hopeless

Silly me
for thinking I could be loved,
that I could be worth more
than your breadcrumbs.
Silly me
for having hope,
for waiting,
for wanting
human connection.
Silly me
for thinking this wouldn't end in rejection.

Evil Eye

I was sitting under a tree
when an overweight woman walked by with her overweight friend
and glared at me.
Skinny me,
underweight from homelessness,
sitting there in a dress and black leggings.
How fucking dare I exist.
Stung by her hatred,
I made an annoyed expression.
So she walked up to me,
and stood over me,
and stared at me.
She was trying to intimidate me,
or challenge me to a fight.
I don't think she realized how tall I was,
sitting down as I was,
and that I wasn't frightened of her wee height.
With bulging yoga arms and legs,
I could have beat her ass for days.
But she thought she was intimidating me.
How cute.
I stared into her ugly face,
my face twisted,
I stared
like she was crazy.
She was fat,
and her eyes were beady,
and her brown hair was thin and limp.
But it was all my fault somehow.
I deserved her blame.
I was the outlet for her shame.
Me, the hated thin woman,

who happened to just be sitting there minding my business.
I have only ever minded my business,
but jealous women persist.
It was cold,
so half my face was hidden by a scarf
against the wind.
But this woman and her friend,
just stood there
like I was supposed to care.
She couldn't tell that I was annoyed.
In her warped mind, I was probably "frightened."
Eventually, I just went back to scrolling through my phone and ignored her.
She walked off smiling with her friend,
as if she had accomplished something,
as if she had successfully intimidated someone she was envious of.
But all she did
was show how immature,
self-hating,
and toxic she was.
So I wish the best for her.
I hope one day she loses weight.
I hope one day she makes her hair look nice,
that she "glows up,"
that men start lining up for her.
Then all her fat friends will leave her,
will randomly hate her,
will compete with her,
will forsake her—
And then she'll look back on the day she tried to fight the skinny woman under the tree,
she'll look back and she'll realize
what it's like to be me.

Lavender Flower

I feel you,
even when you're far away,
I feel you,
and a day
doesn't go by when I don't think of you and smile.
I feel your arms close around me,
and I turn and straddle your lap.
My breasts crush you
as I enclose you in my arms.
You love how full they are,
you love the strength
of my thighs around you.
You are trapped
but you like being caught
in my heat,
in my softness,
in the scent of my cocoa butter skin,
lost within my eyes.
My thighs
tighten,
holding you in place,
you can't escape,
you are mine.
My slender fingers
push through your hair,
and my eyes soften as I look at you,
and I kiss you,
I taste your lips,
your hands grip my hips,
and all the world stands still
as we express this love
blossoming bright in our hearts—

My butch lavender flower,
what is this power
you have over me?

I Walk Alone

And I don't know
what love is,
but I know it doesn't hurt.
It isn't pining for someone
who doesn't see my worth.
It isn't hoping in vain
for crumbs of affection.
It isn't tears and sadness
from vague, lowkey rejection.
If you truly wanted me,
I wouldn't have to wonder.
I wouldn't have to wait,
and I wouldn't have to blunder.
None of it is your fault,
and you are free to make your choice.
Yet I wish I'd never met you,
wish I'd never heard your voice,
wish I'd never looked into your eyes,
wish I'd never dared to hope
that you could actually choose me back,
that I wouldn't have to mope.
It seems I walk this endless road
isolated and alone,
the outcast who no woman wants,
always rejected and on my own.
Again, that's not your fault,
so I will spare my wrath.
Go forth, forget me,
move on, be gone.
Leave me to walk my lonely path.

Nutter Butters

A pigeon tried to sit on my hand this morning.
I think they remember me,
the homeless woman,
who giggles at how cute and fat they are,
who sometimes tosses junk food—
tasty hot Fritos, Doritos, Ruffles—
Hey, I try to give the pigeons apples
but they do not want them.
They're as addicted to that dopamine hit as I.
I think they're getting fat off me,
but I can't stop feeding them.
And why not?
Today it was Nutter Butters. They went wild.
I smiled as I watched them, laughed at the cookie crumbs on their beaks.
Poor pigeons, with no hands to wipe the crumbs away.
To the random observer,
they probably think I'm lonely,
yet I'm perfectly content
living only
to feed the pigeons.
Outcast? Yes. Loner? Yes. But I've made peace with it.
I am not lonely.
This has always been the pattern of my life,
even before homelessness,
me,
alone, shunned, unwanted—
But animals, somehow, animals always come.
I don't have to throw food every time.
Sometimes the pigeons just come and sit beside me.
It is more than any human has ever done.
Except for you.
You're the only person who's ever . . .

sat beside me when I needed it,
comforted me when I needed it,
refused to abandon me when I was upset.
And I can't forget
that day.
Your hand on my back as I wept,
and you promised you would go away
if I asked,
but I didn't ask.
Alone, solitary, on my own
for thirty-six years,
thirty-six years . . .
And you were the first human I *wanted* to sit beside me,
I wanted to stay,
I wanted to keep.
Surely that must mean something?
Or maybe it means nothing,
and I really am just
lonely.
Nutter Butters taste better
when there's someone to share them with,
when there's someone to lick the peanutbutter off your hands.
It's just not the same . . .
when you lick your own fingers.

Think of Me

When the darkness leaves you lonely,
when you feel adrift at sea,
when you feel that yearning growing—
Darling,
stop and think of me.
When the moon seems sad and hollow
when the stars above collide,
when your world is painful and uncertain,
and there's no one on your side,
Just you stop and close your eyes,
I am right there in your dreams,
walking, shielding, protecting,
I was with you all along.

Petals

I put a rose between my thighs
and think of you.
It seems wrong,
but I see it through.
The rose is plastic,
a toy,
but I pretend it is you.
The rose is your mouth
and your stems are slow and firm,
gliding so deep inside,
and your petals
caressing my petals –
They're soft
and wet
and hot.
They suck at my helpless flower,
softness to softness,
in the deepest kiss,
and I melt into the sheets,
thighs spread,
wondering how you did this.
How you hijacked my mind,
invaded my fantasies.
I can't forget your eyes.
Oh, I've tried.
Believe me, I've tried.
Petals pooling across the bed
in swirls of moonlight and starlight.
And as I climax under your kiss,
it feels right.
My body craves you,
but so does my soul.

I love you.
Did you hear that?
I love you.
Don't ever let go.

Forget About Love

I remember a time when I craved love,
prayed for love,
thought I would be saved by love.
Now I don't care at all.
I'm not sure I even
believe in it,
this corny *thing* from the Disney movies.
I am Jasmine,
forgetting about love,
except there's no Iago to trick me
back into Aladdin's arms.
I am Megara,
jaded and done.
I don't want to be part of your world.
I don't need anyone.
Let me sleep without assault –
I mean, True Love's kiss,
And don't try to save me from the burning tower that is my life.
Move along.
I got this.

5/5

Darling,
you are five for five.
Five times we have spoken,
fives times did Cupid's Arrow
hit the bull's eye.
Five times I
ran,
tried to avoid,
dodged and ducked,
felt annoyed.
But it's useless,
and I am done.
Five times out of five,
you've surely won.
Darling, darling,
I surrender.
Please be tender
when you claim your victim.
A ten out of ten,
you are beautiful,
with satin skin
and intense eyes.
Then you look at me,
and I ...
Speechless, I.

I Am Someone

Homelessness
is an ego-wrecking nightmare.
All your dignity is stripped away,
until you discover you are nothing,
you are no one—
I am nothing,
I am no one.
I am
a spec of dust
drifting through the Universe,
indistinguishable from the other specs—
NO!
I am God,
master of my final destiny,
spinning worlds into being with words—
I am She
who lights the dark.
I *am* the dark,
burning away all the light—
I am the night.
I am the day.
I am the sun.
I am the moon.
I am the stars—
Yet to you I am nothing—
Nothing! –
but a worthless homeless woman,
someone to look down on
so that YOU can feel better.
I have no value
except what's between my legs,
so keep badgering me for sex

and act surprised when I lash out in anger –
I am a stranger
passing in the night
who you cross the street to avoid.
I am annoyed
when you disrespect and mistreat me,
but I have no right to my rage,
for I am no one,
I am nothing,
I am the roach under your boot.
You sneer as you speak to me,
for I am a bug—
NO.
I am the moon.
I am the stars.
I am someone.
I AM SOMEONE.
And you will not take that away.

Codependent No More

I keep waiting for the feeling to go away,
but it persists.
I love you.
I love you.
I love you.
Like a heartbeat,
it goes on and on.
I love you.
Yet I suffer not.
I do not say the words in agony.
There is no angst.
No suffering.
Just bliss.
I love you,
and
it doesn't matter
if we never kiss.
I love you,
and
I want you to be happy.
Without reason or rhyme,
without longing,
without pain,
I love you!
And there is no standing in the rain.
Because I can love you
without chasing you,
without expecting to gain.
I love you,
and
you aren't expected
to feel the same.

I'll Steal You

I want to steal you,
take you away from your busy life
for an hour or two
and hold you close in my arms,
let time stand still,
stroke your hair
and listen to the rain.
Just for a little while,
just for a little while,
I would keep you
and oh, you would be mine.
Just for a moment,
to kiss you,
to love you,
just for a moment,
for a moment in time.

Mine

What have you done to me?
I can not speak.
The words,
words
melt to moans in my mouth.
My body craves you,
craves you
all the time.
Would that I could bind you to me
and really make you,
make you
mine.

Camila 2

Camila,
curvy and short,
wants her money NOW!
Camila,
sitting next to me
like a giant doll.
Camila,
too curvy to be real,
spreading her thighs
and arching her heels.
Camila
always speaks Spanish
because fuck English.
Camila,
hips moving with a swing.
Camila,
tastes like nothing
and everything.
Camila,
hot and soft and wet.
Camila,
I won't soon forget.
Camila,
thinks I have a pretty name.
Camila,
I will come again.

Camila

The room was dark.
The apartment was dark.
As if to hide her face
while she revealed nonetheless her most intimate places.
She kept speaking Spanish to me.
I was nervous.
I fumbled to pay her through CashApp.
Then she took off her robe
and revealed her beautiful body.
She was soft
and wet
and I didn't want it to end.
She pretended at first
but soon, her moans of delight became real.
And as her pleasure mounted
so did mine.
As I fumbled to put my bra on,
she told me I was good.
She asked for my name.
I was surprised but I told her.
She said in Spanish that my name was pretty.
I said "thank you" in Spanish.
The transaction complete,
I walked down the street,
smiling,
Thinking of her heat against my face
and how I wanted to go down on her for a hundred years.
I felt like a vampire,
my lust for sweetness awakened.
And I wished I had a
girlfriend who looked like her,
a perfect hourglass

with long black hair.
I will never forget
her fingers in my hair
as she grinded herself against my face.
And the taste of her.
Sweet, soft, and wet is woman.
This is the thing men covet,
this center of all life,
this little death,
this ecstasy between two quivering thighs.
A woman can only
belong to herself.
Yet I wanted her for myself.
I,
So clumsy and awkwardly built.
I wanted her to want ugly me.
What must it feel like
to be wanted
to be seen
for just who you are?
What is it like to make love to someone who loves you?
Perhaps I will never know.
But I know the taste of a woman,
her softness,
her sweetness.
And perhaps that is enough.

Self-Acceptance

I gained weight,
became puffy and irate.
And I loved her.
My sadness is dangerous;
it often turns to anger.
And I loved her.
I cut off my hair;
made myself ugly and bare.
And I loved her.
I did everything in my power
to abandon myself.
And I loved her.
When all the world was against me,
I loved her.

Don't miss out!

Visit the website below and you can sign up to receive emails whenever Lee Gray publishes a new book. There's no charge and no obligation.

https://books2read.com/r/B-A-DGRK-XRJCC

BOOKS 2 READ

Connecting independent readers to independent writers.

Did you love *Phoenix Rising*? Then you should read *Shit I'm Tired of Saying*[1] by Lee Gray!

[2]

The unapologetic awakening of a radical black lesbian feminist. Read more at https://www.instagram.com/leegpoet/.

1. https://books2read.com/u/49D8K0

2. https://books2read.com/u/49D8K0

Also by Lee Gray

That Time a Fish Loved a Bird
Shit I'm Tired of Saying
What They Didn't Teach Yo Ass in School
All That is Love
She is (Not) my King
Sick of You and Everything
Phoenix Rising

Watch for more at https://www.instagram.com/leegpoet/.

Adobe Stock | #119935266

About the Author

Lee is a lesbian who lives in California.

Read more at https://www.instagram.com/leegpoet/.

www.ingramcontent.com/pod-product-compliance
Lightning Source LLC
LaVergne TN
LVHW010501160826
845677LV00012B/2591